T0198420

You Are Soooo Loved

Caitlin E. Stevens

To order additional copies of this book, contact:
Xlibris
844-714-8691
www.Xlibris.com
Orders@Xlibris.com

ISBN: Softcover   978-1-6641-8220-2
        Hardcover   978-1-6641-8221-9
        EBook   978-1-6641-8219-6

Print information available on the last page

Rev. date: 06/28/2021

In memory of my mom, who always made sure I knew just how much I was loved 🩶

Dearest Little One,
Have I told you how much you're loved? Well, let's take some time to see the ways. I love you so much! In fact, my love for you is...

More

Colorful

Than a rainbow spanning across the sky

Than a sunset
at the end of the day

Warmer

Than rays of sunlight
shining down from
the midday sun

Deeper

Than the
bottom of the ocean floor

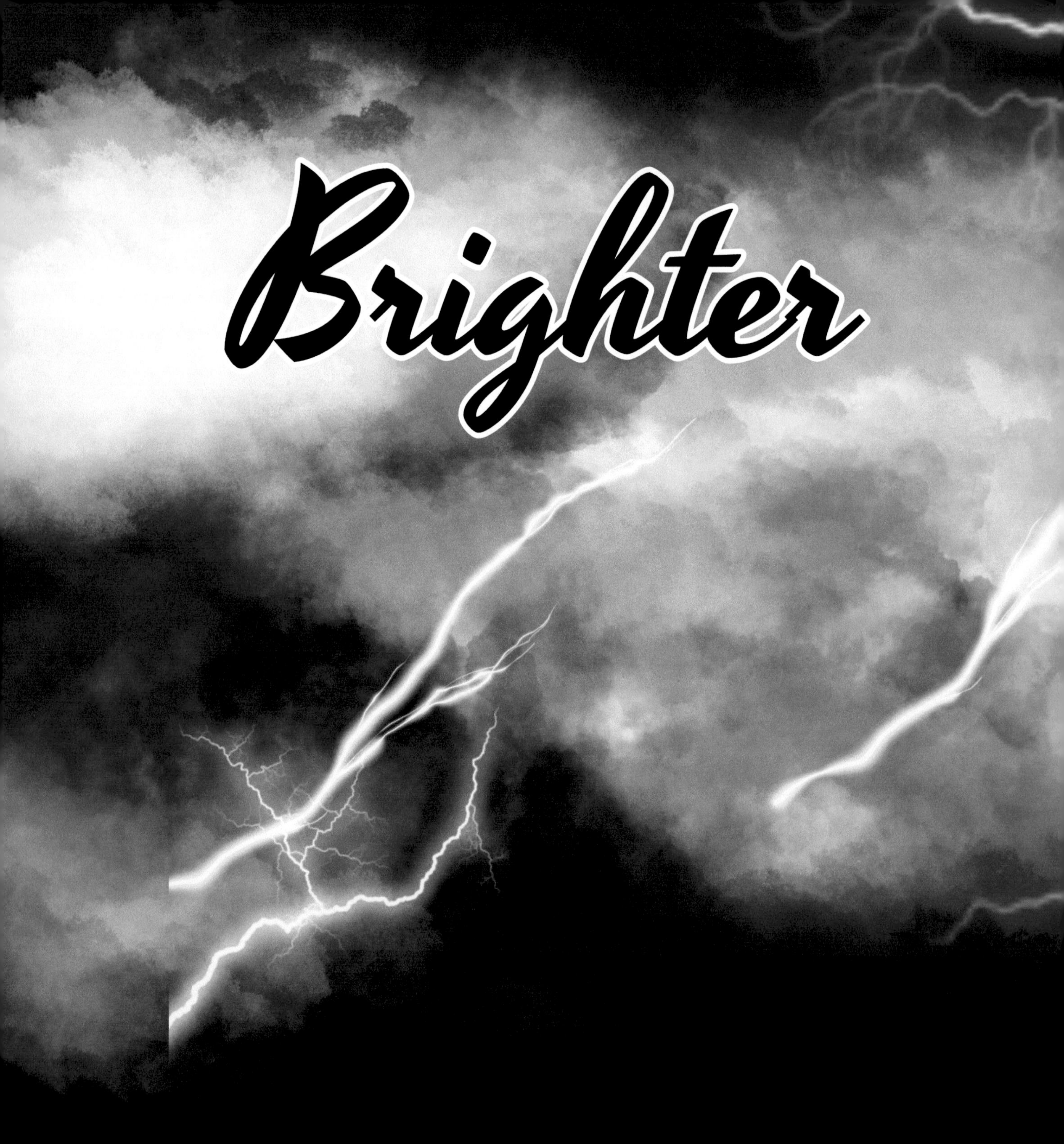
Brighter

Than a flash of lightening amongst a dark stormy sky

More

Unique

Than a single fallen
snowflake
compared to all of the rest

Than a teeny tiny butterfly

More
Plentiful

Than all of the grains of sand on an island beach

Richer

Than all of the money and jewels in the world combined

Than the ripest summer strawberry

My love for you is just as
PERFECT

As
YOU ARE!!

I want you
to know

You are
Cherished

You are
Beautiful

You are
Loved

Printed in the United States
by Baker & Taylor Publisher Services